# GOING UNDERGROUND

**Buffy Silverman**

**Chicago, Illinois**

© 2007 Raintree
Published by Raintree,
A division of Reed Elsevier Inc.
Chicago, Illinois

Customer Service  888-363-4266

Visit our website at www.heinemannraintree.com

Designed by Michelle Lisseter and
Bridge Creative Services.
Picture research by Hannah Taylor and Fiona Orbell.
Printed and bound in China by WKT
Company Limited.

11 10 09 08 07
10 9 8 7 6 5 4 3 2 1

**Library of Congress Cataloging-in-
Publication Data**
Silverman, Buffy.
  Going underground / Buffy Silverman.
      p. cm.
  Includes bibliographical references and index.
  ISBN 1-4109-2598-6 (library binding-hardcover) --
ISBN 1-4109-2627-3 (pbk.)
  1.  Municipal engineering--Juvenile literature.  I.
Title.
  TD159.3.S55 2006
  628--dc22
                                          2006008786

13-digit ISBNs
978-1-4109-2598-5 (hardcover)
978-1-4109-2627-2 (paperback)

**Acknowledgments**
The author and publisher are grateful to the
following for permission to reproduce copyright
material: Alamy Images pp. **4–5** (Chad Ehlers),
**14–15** (Frances Roberts), **18–19** (Glyn Thomas),
**16–17** (Michelle Chaplow), **22** (Rodolfo Arpia);
Alamy Images/ACE STOCK LIMITED p. **23**; Alamy
Images/qaphotos.com pp. **6–7**; Corbis p. **11** (Lester
Lefkowitz), **8–9** (Tom Stewart), **12** (William Taufic);
Corbis/Underwood & Underwood pp. **24–25**;
Corbis/zuma/Art Stein p. **24** inset; Getty Images/The
Image Bank p. **10**; Istockphoto.com p. **21** (Brian
Stanback); The NEMO Program p. **20** (Kara Bonsack).

Cover photograph of glowing manhole
with cover reproduced with permission of
Photolibrary.com/Index Stock Imagery.

Illustrations by Bridge Creative Services.

The publishers would like to thank Nancy Harris and
Daniel Block for their assistance in the preparation of
this book.

# Contents

Some words are printed in bold, **like this**. You can find out what they mean on page 30. You can also look in the box at the bottom of the page where they first appear.

# Going Underground!

Look up in a city. Very tall buildings called skyscrapers surround you. How do heat and water get into these buildings? How do they get electricity (power)? The skyscrapers are heavy. How do they stay standing?

You will not find the answers to these questions by looking above you. The answers are hidden underground. A city that rises up high into the sky begins deep underground.

*In a city, some buildings ▶ soar to the sky. But what happens under the ground?*

4

Let's take a look at the hidden world under our feet. Let's look beneath a city.

# Under the Street

Let's start our underground tour. We travel down from the surface of the street. About 2 feet (0.6 meters) below, we reach the first pipes. They are buried beneath the side of the street. These pipes hold electric **cables**. A cable is made of a wire or a group of wires that are wrapped together. The wires are made of a reddish-brown metal. The metal is copper. Electricity (power) flows through the wires.

Where has the electricity come from? Electricity is made at a **power plant**. The electricity travels from the power plant through cables. Cables bring electricity to every building in a city.

## Where are the wires?

Sometimes cables are strung above ground on telephone poles. But on crowded city streets, there is no room for telephone poles. That is why the cables are buried in pipes under the street.

**cable**          wire or group of wires that are wrapped together

▼ Electric cables run through pipes. These pipes are buried beneath the street. Workers go under the street to fix the electric cables.

# Let's talk!

Next to the electric **cables**, we find other pipes. Telephone wires are inside of them.

If you want to call a friend, you pick up the telephone and dial. The phone rings in your friend's house. Your friend picks up the phone. You start to talk. How do your voices travel to each other?

Your telephone cord is plugged into a **phone jack**. The phone jack is in the wall. A pair of wires runs from the phone jack through the walls of your house. One wire sends your message to your friend. The other wire brings your friend's voice back to you.

*When you speak on the ▶ telephone, a signal is sent through telephone wires. Telephone wires are often buried beneath the street.*

**phone jack**   special plug for a telephone

The wires connect to a box outside your home. From the box, your phone wires go under the street. The wires go to a phone company. When you dial a friend's number, your phone lines are connected at the phone company. Signals travel back and forth along the wires.

# Staying warm

Now we travel 3 feet (1 meter) below the street. Beneath the electrical and telephone pipes is another pipe. **Natural gas** flows through it.

What is natural gas? It is a **fuel**. People burn fuel to get energy (power). The energy from natural gas heats and cools buildings. Natural gas is also used for cooking. **Power plants** use natural gas to make electricity.

*When you turn on the ▼ stove, flames heat a pan. The stove burns natural gas to make heat.*

| | |
|---|---|
| **fuel** | something used to make energy |
| **natural gas** | gas that can be burned to make energy |
| **pipeline** | system of pipes through which water or gas flow |

*A worker turns a wheel. ▼ They control the flow of natural gas through pipes.*

Natural gas travels far before it reaches a city building. People drill deep in the ground to find natural gas. If there is gas underground, it rises to the surface. It flows into large **pipelines**. Pipelines are systems of many pipes.

Pipelines can carry natural gas hundreds of miles. The pipelines carry gas to where people use it. In a city, natural gas moves through pipelines beneath the streets.

# Where is the Water?

As we move farther below the street, we find a larger pipe. Water flows through it.

We use water every day. We need clean water for drinking. We need clean water for cooking and washing. Water also flushes a toilet.

▼ Water flows through a treatment plant, where it is cleaned.

| main | large underground pipe that carries water, gas, or steam |
| reservoir | human-made lake used for storing water |

A city may get water from a lake or river. It may get water from the ground, or from a large, human-made lake called a **reservoir**. Pumps push this water to a **treatment plant**. Water is cleaned at the treatment plant.

Then, the clean water flows through pipes. These pipes are called **mains**. Water mains are buried underground.

Smaller pipes branch off a water main. They bring water into buildings. Water flows through pipes in the walls of buildings. The pipes connect to faucets, such as those found in sinks. You turn a faucet. Water flows out.

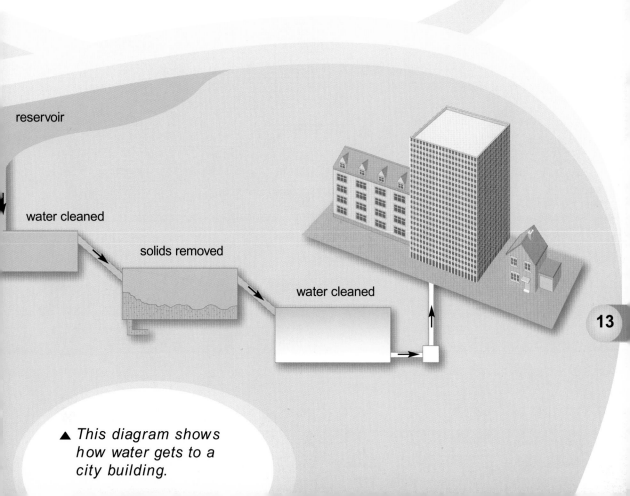

reservoir

water cleaned

solids removed

water cleaned

▲ *This diagram shows how water gets to a city building.*

**manhole**   hole through which a person can enter an underground system

**valve**   object that controls water flowing through a pipe

# In a manhole

Sometimes water pipes leak or break. How do workers fix broken pipes? They must go under the street. They climb down to special underground rooms. The holes in the ground leading to these rooms are called **manholes**.

On the street level, a heavy lid covers the entrance. To enter the manhole, a worker removes the cover. Then, the worker climbs down the manhole.

A large underground water **main** runs through the underground room. Attached to the water main is a **valve**. A valve controls the flow of water. A worker turns the valve. The valve lowers a gate inside the water main. The gate blocks the water. The water stops flowing through the main. Once the water is shut off, the pipe can be fixed.

◄ *Have you ever seen someone climb down a manhole? The person disappears under the street.*

# Steam power

Let's go farther down. We are 6 feet (about 2 meters) below ground. We are in the middle of the street. We see another pipe. Hot steam travels through it. Steam is the gas that forms when water is boiled.

This pipe looks different. It is shaped like a square, not a circle. That is because concrete covers the round metal pipe. Concrete is a material made from sand and gravel. Steam makes the pipe very hot. The concrete keeps the heat inside the pipe.

Where does the steam go? In big cities, many buildings use steam for heat. Pipes carry steam under busy streets. Smaller pipes branch off the **main** pipe. The smaller pipes bring steam into buildings.

## Steamy city

*New York City uses a lot of steam. Every year, 30 billion pounds (14 billion kilograms) of steam flows beneath the city's streets.*

▼ Sometimes steam leaks from a pipe. When the steam hits cool air, it makes a cloud. On a city street, you might see steam rising out of a **manhole** cover.

# Getting Rid of Waste

Now, let's go really far down. We are now more than 10 feet (3 meters) below the street. Here we find a **sewer** tunnel. Every city must get rid of **wastewater** (dirty water). Sewer tunnels carry wastewater away.

When you wash your hands, dirty water flows down the drain. When you flush the toilet, water and waste swirl away. Wastewater flows through indoor pipes. It leaves the building. It empties into a sewer tunnel under the street.

Sewer pipes from several small streets join a larger pipe. Larger pipes also join together. The largest pipe is called a sewer **main**. It carries wastewater to another **treatment plant**. The wastewater is cleaned at the treatment plant.

*Huge sewer tunnels run deep ▶ below the street. Wastewater flows through the tunnels.*

**sewer**    system of underground pipes that carries dirty water

# In a storm drain

We have reached the deepest underground pipe. It is below all the other pipes in the street. This pipe is much larger than a **sewer** pipe. It is a **storm drain**.

When rain falls or snow melts, water flows down city streets. Huge puddles form. Without a place to go, storm water would flood streets and buildings. Where does rainwater go? It empties into a storm drain.

▼ Rain rushes down a street. It flows into an opening on the side of the street. The opening leads to a storm drain under the street.

**polluted**    dirty
**storm drain**    pipe that carries rainwater away from a city street

During a big storm, a storm drain carries a lot of water. This storm drain is emptying into a lake.

Trash from our streets is swept into the storm drain. The trash makes the water dirty. It makes the water **polluted**.

Some storm drains empty into rivers, lakes, or oceans. Other storm drains join sewer pipes.

# Below a Building

Let's go deeper down under the **storm drain**. We now find the supports that hold up tall city buildings.

A tall building needs a strong bottom. The bottom is called the **foundation**. A foundation supports the building's weight. The foundation is below the ground.

When workers build a skyscraper, they start with the foundation. They dig a hole deep underground. They make the foundation strong by using tough materials. Rods made of a strong metal, such as **steel**, support a building. Sand and gravel are mixed to make concrete. The concrete is poured over the steel.

*The foundation of a ▼ skyscraper must be strong. It supports the weight of a heavy building.*

22

| | |
|---|---|
| **foundation** | part of a building below ground |
| **steel** | strong, hard kind of metal |

◀ *The lights of the Petronas Towers glow at night. The towers have 32,000 windows! A sky bridge connects the two towers.*

## Weighty towers

*The Petronas Towers in Malaysia are 88 stories (floors) tall. Their huge concrete foundations go down 400 feet (122 meters) below ground. These foundations hold up the heavy towers.*

# Traveling Underground

Where can you find people underground? Let's go beneath the pipes in a street. Then, let's take a ride on a **subway**!

Subway trains run on tracks through underground tunnels. The tunnels are built below city streets and buildings.

A subway car carries ▼ riders from one station to the next. The cars take people all over the city.

## Subway firsts

The London Underground is the world's oldest subway. It opened in 1863.

**elevator**   device that can move people from one level to another

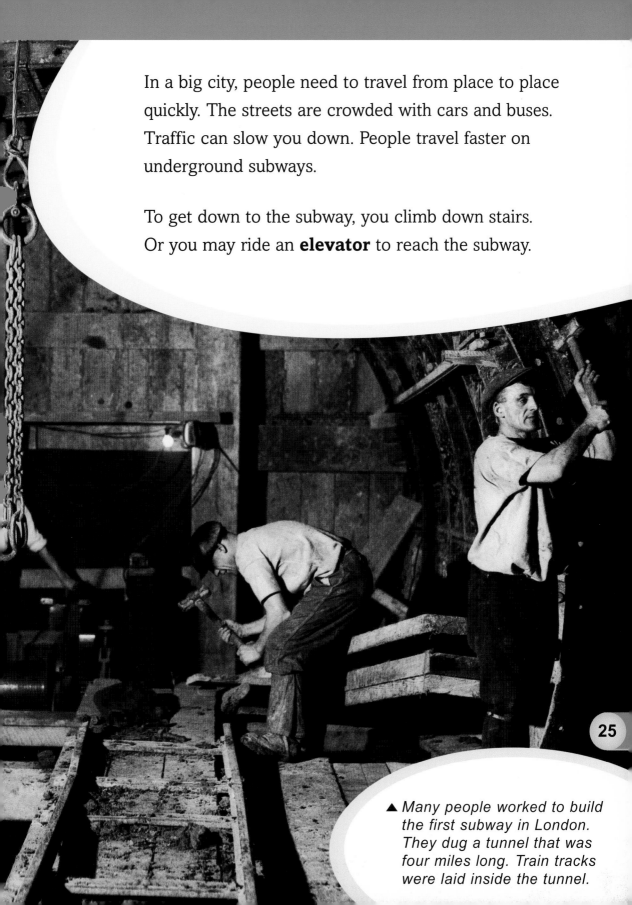

In a big city, people need to travel from place to place quickly. The streets are crowded with cars and buses. Traffic can slow you down. People travel faster on underground subways.

To get down to the subway, you climb down stairs. Or you may ride an **elevator** to reach the subway.

25

▲ *Many people worked to build the first subway in London. They dug a tunnel that was four miles long. Train tracks were laid inside the tunnel.*

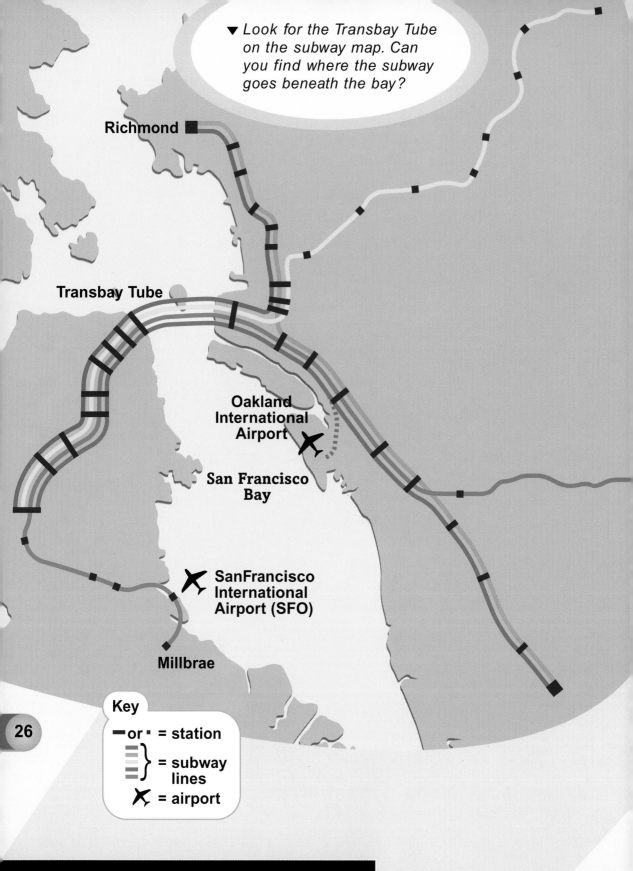

▼ *Look for the Transbay Tube on the subway map. Can you find where the subway goes beneath the bay?*

**Richmond** ■

**Transbay Tube**

**Oakland International Airport** ✈

**San Francisco Bay**

✈ **SanFrancisco International Airport (SFO)**

**Millbrae**

**Key**
— or ▪ = station
} = subway lines
✈ = airport

**bay** body of water partly surrounded by land

# Under a bay

How does a **subway** car cross water? It can go above ground on a bridge. It can also go beneath the water in a tunnel.

The San Francisco **Bay** is in California. A bay is a body of water partly surrounded by land. The world's longest underwater subway travels beneath the San Francisco Bay. Trains cross under the bay through the Transbay Tube. Transbay means *across the bay*. The underwater tube is 3.6 miles (5.8 kilometers) long.

A bridge also crosses the San Francisco Bay. But the bridge is usually crowded with cars. By traveling under the bay in the subway, people can cross more quickly.

## Building underwater

*In 1965, workers started the Transbay Tube. The tube was built in pieces. A boat towed each section into the San Francisco Bay. The sections were lowered into a deep ditch at the bottom.*

# What is Underground?

In a city many things travel underground. Electricity travels underground. So do phone lines, **fuel** (such as natural gas) and water. They travel through pipes beneath a street. When people travel they often ride underground in a **subway** train.

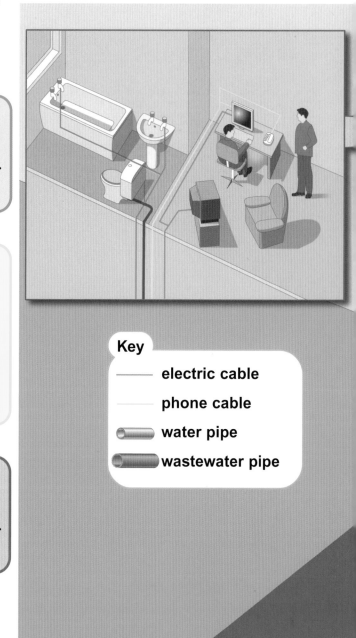

## How does electricity enter a building?
Electricity is made in a **power plant**. It travels through electric **cables**.

## How does your friend's voice travel back to you?
You call a friend. A signal travels from your phone. It travels through a phone wire. The wire connects with phone wires under the street. Your friend answers.

## Where does dirty water go?
**Wastewater** flows down a drain. It leaves the building through a pipe. The pipe connects to a **sewer** pipe.

**Key**
_____ electric cable
_____ phone cable
▭ water pipe
▭ wastewater pipe

### Where does water come from?

City water often comes from a large lake. The lake is called a **reservoir**. Water leaves the reservoir. It flows through pipes under the street. Pipes bring water to a building.

# Glossary

**bay**  body of water partly surrounded by land

**cable**  wire or group of wires that are wrapped together

**elevator**  device that can move people from one level to another. You can use an elevator to reach the subway from the sidewalk.

**foundation**  part of a building below ground. The foundation supports the weight of a building.

**fuel**  something used to make energy. Coal, oil, and gas are fuels.

**main**  large underground pipe that carries water, gas, or steam

**manhole**  hole through which a person can enter an underground system. Workers fix pipes by going underground through a manhole.

**natural gas**  gas that can be burned to make energy. People use natural gas for heating, cooling, cooking, and making electricity.

**phone jack**  special plug for a telephone. A telephone cord plugs into a phone jack.

**pipeline**  system of pipes through which water or gas flow. Pipelines often stretch hundreds of miles.

**polluted**  dirty. Polluted water is harmful to drink or bathe in.

**power plant**  place where electricity is made. Electricity travels from a power plant to where people need it.

**reservoir**  human-made lake used for storing water. A city's reservoir may be far away.

**sewer**  system of underground pipes that carries dirty water. A sewer system takes dirty water away from the city.

**steel**  strong, hard kind of metal. The foundation of a tall building is made with steel rods.

**storm drain**  pipe that carries rainwater away from a city street

**subway**  train that travels underground

**treatment plant**  place for cleaning water. Water can then be sent to homes and offices.

**valve**  object that controls water flowing through a pipe

**wastewater**  water mixed with waste. Wastewater is carried away through the sewer system.

# Want to Know More?

## Books to read

- Hopkinson, Deborah. *Sky Boys: How They Built the Empire State Building.* New York: Random House, 2006.

- Parker, Steve. *Electricity* (DK Eyewitness Books). New York: DK Children, 2005.

## Website

- http://www.nationalgeographic.com/3cities/
  Compare three cities. Look at how city life has changed over the last 2,000 years.

- http://www.skyscraper.org/
  Learn more about skyscrapers at the Skyscraper Museum's website. Try clicking on Cool Stuff for Kids.

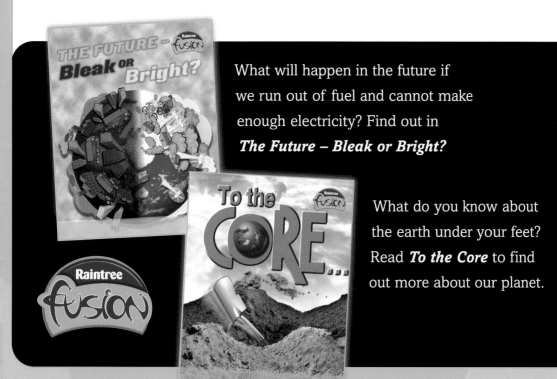

What will happen in the future if we run out of fuel and cannot make enough electricity? Find out in *The Future – Bleak or Bright?*

What do you know about the earth under your feet? Read *To the Core* to find out more about our planet.

# Index